An Imprint of Pop!
popbooksonline.com

Ancient Mythologies

HINDU MYTHOLOGY

by Elizabeth Andrews

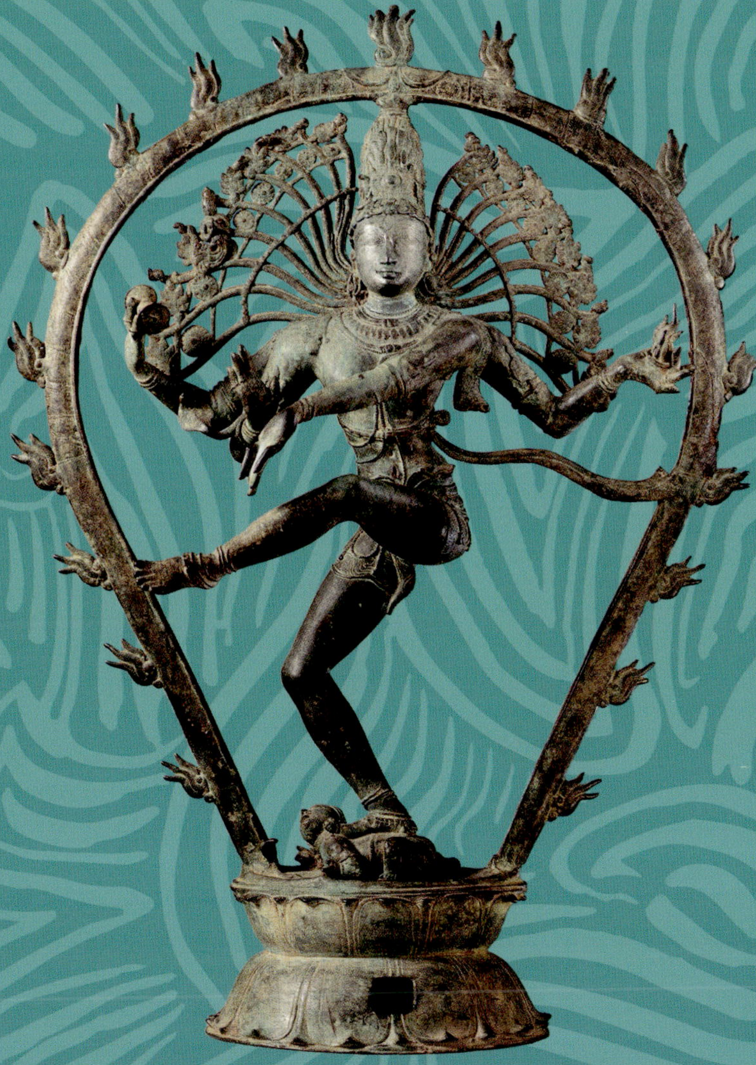

WELCOME TO DiscoverRoo!

This book is filled with videos, puzzles, games, and more! Scan the QR codes* while you read, or visit the website below to make this book pop.

popbooksonline.com/hindu-myth

abdobooks.com

Published by Pop!, a division of ABDO, PO Box 398166, Minneapolis, Minnesota 55439.

Printed in the United States of America, North Mankato, Minnesota.

102024
012025

Cover Photo: Getty Images

Interior Photos: Getty Images, Shutterstock Images, Wikimedia Commons, Wikimedia Commons/TAPAS KUMAR HALDER

Editor: Krissy Sterling

Series Designer: Colleen McLaren

Library of Congress Control Number: 2024938607

Publisher's Cataloging-in-Publication Data

Names: Andrews, Elizabeth, author.

Title: Hindu mythology / by Elizabeth Andrews

Description: Minneapolis, Minnesota : Pop!, 2025 | Series: Ancient mythologies | Includes online resources and index

Identifiers: ISBN 9781098247041 (lib. bdg.) | ISBN 9781098247607 (ebook)

Subjects: LCSH: Mythology--Juvenile literature. | Hindu mythology--Juvenile literature. | Hindu gods--Juvenile literature. | Deities--Juvenile literature. | Mythology, Asian--Juvenile literature.

Classification: DDC 294.51--dc23

*Scanning QR codes requires a web-enabled smart device with a QR code reader app and a camera.

TABLE OF CONTENTS

CHAPTER 1

NOT THE FIRST UNIVERSE

At the beginning, before the world existed as we know it, there was Brahman. Brahman is without form or body and cannot be described with human words. Brahman is the **universe** itself. Our universe is trillions of years old. It is not the first universe, and it will not be the last.

WATCH A VIDEO HERE!

Hindus believe that everyone exists in a cycle of birth, death, and rebirth. The cycle is called samsara.

Gods are constantly at war with demons in Hindu mythology.

Hindu mythology says there have been many universes before ours and there will be many universes after. The history of our current universe is divided into four yugas. Each yuga is shorter than the last. They are measured in divine years. A divine year is equal to 432,000 human years.

The first yuga was a nearly perfect time. It lasted 4,000 divine years. Humans were giants. They were good, kind, and truthful. The second yuga was 3,000 divine years. Humans were intelligent, but they had lost a quarter of their truth. They were less good and less kind.

The third yuga lasted 2,000 divine years. Humans lost half of their truth. They were evil and cared about power more than knowledge. We are in the fourth yuga. It began in 3102 BCE. It is the darkest yuga, as humans have harmful emotions such as hatred and greed. When this yuga ends, the world will be destroyed, and a new universe cycle will begin.

Other mythologies have creation stories that begin with an egg too.

The first man was named Manu.

The power of the universe interacts with the world through three beings. They are Brahma, Shiva, and Vishnu. Brahma is the creator god. He was born from an egg. When he emerged from the egg, he created good and evil and light and dark. Next Brahma made gods, demons, humans, and all living beings.

The lotus flower connected to Vishnu's belly button contains life energy.

There are different stories of creation in Hindu mythology. Another story says Brahma was born from Vishnu's belly button. Brahma created the heavens, earth, and sky. Then, he split himself in two to create man and woman.

Nearly every society has a creation myth. Myths are stories that often involve gods and **supernatural** events. They are not always based in fact. Myths helped people make sense of the world around them.

Hinduism is a religion full of characters and color.

CHAPTER 2

BRAHMA, SHIVA, VISHNU

Brahma, Shiva, and Vishnu are each a form of the **universe**. They all play a very important role in the cycle of existence in Hindu mythology. Brahma, Shiva, and Vishnu interact with the world as avatars. Avatars are different forms gods take on.

LEARN MORE HERE!

One of Vishnu's avatars, Krishna, plays a flute.

The items carried by each god are important to their roles.

Brahma creates each universe. He likes to spend his time meditating, or focusing on breath and clearing the mind. Brahma exists in everything because he created it all.

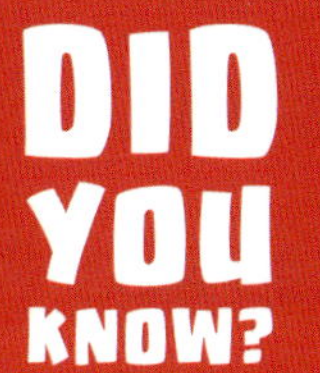

Many mythologies have a story about a great flood.

Vishnu is the **preserver**. He is a kind god who cares for and protects humans. His avatars show up to give humans guidance or assist in fighting. Vishnu's avatars are some of the most popular gods in Hindu mythology. His first avatar was Matsya. He was half fish. Matsya saved many living creatures from a great flood.

Matsya was caught as a small fish by the first human. Matsya grew to a giant size.

Shiva is the destroyer god. He is not a scary god though. Shiva exists so new things can grow. He is **merciful**. Shiva always protects the weak. His animal avatar is a white bull called Nandi. Nandi once cursed an evil demon king named Ravana.

Shiva is often shown with animal skins. This represents his victories over the strongest forces.

Brahma and Vishnu once argued about which of them was more powerful. Shiva appeared at the argument as a **pillar** of fire. Neither Brahma nor Vishnu could reach the bottom or top of the pillar. They agreed that their failure proved Shiva to be more powerful than either of them.

This statue depicts Shiva as the Lord of Dance.

CHAPTER 3

MORE GODS AND GODDESSES

There may be millions of gods and goddesses in Hindu mythology. Some are forms of Brahma, Vishnu, and Shiva. Others are their children or created from nature. These gods are a part of many Hindu myths.

EXPLORE LINKS HERE!

The Hindu goddess of music is named Sarasvati.

GODS AND GODDESSES

Different types of Hindus **worship** different gods. Ancient Hindus worshipped by praying and performing **rituals** at sites dedicated to their god.

Shiva

Lakshmi

Vishnu

Ganesha

Parvati

Kali

Brahma

Parvati is a goddess born from a mountain called Himalaya. She is the goddess of marriage, family, beauty, **fertility**, and the arts. She is married to Shiva. They have two children named Ganesha and Skanda. Ganesha is a god with the head of an elephant. Parvati made Ganesha from mud to guard her while she bathed.

Parvati was created to be Shiva's wife.

DID YOU KNOW?

Skanda is the god of war. He has six faces.

Keeping a statue of Ganesha in a home brings peace and balance.

When Shiva came home and saw a strange boy near his wife, he cut off Ganesha's head. Shiva regretted his actions. He gave the boy the head of an elephant as a replacement. Hindus pray to Ganesha when they want success.

Durga is also married to Shiva. She is a warrior. Durga was born from flames. She has a fearsome appearance that includes sharp teeth and eight arms. Each arm holds a different weapon. Durga is the goddess of sleep and creativity. It is said she created yoga. Yoga is a very important practice to Hindus.

Kali is another strong goddess. She was born when Durga was fighting a terrible demon. Kali

HINDU DEMONS

Hindu demons were made by Brahma just as humans and gods were. They are often called asuras. Demons are not totally evil, but their goals are often opposite to the goals of gods. This is why there are many stories of Hindu gods battling demons. Demons are more active at night. They are connected to the underworld.

burst from Durga's forehead and killed the demon. She also drank all of its blood before it could be used to create more demons. Kali has a blood-red tongue, fangs, and wears a necklace of skulls.

Durga rides a lion named Dawon.

CHAPTER 4

PRINCE RAMA AND SITA

Vishnu is married to a beautiful goddess named Lakshmi. She is the goddess of fortune, **prosperity**, power, and beauty. She is known for transforming people's greatest dreams into reality.

COMPLETE AN ACTIVITY HERE!

Lakshmi was born from the great flood.

Rama won Sita's hand by bending a bow that no one else could even lift.

An important Hindu myth follows the story of two forms of Vishnu and Lakshmi. Prince Rama was an avatar of Vishnu. He was strong, handsome, and wise. Rama won the hand of the beautiful Princess Sita. She was the avatar of Lakshmi.

After winning Sita's hand, Rama was supposed to take over his father's kingdom. Before that could happen, his evil stepmother sent him and Sita to a dangerous jungle filled with demons called rakshasas.

Rama's brother is named Lakshmana.

Hanuman, the leader of the monkeys, was deeply devoted to Rama.

One of the demons fell in love with Rama. She had Sita kidnapped! Rama and his younger brother went after Sita. She was held captive on an island by Ravana, the king of rakshasas.

To save her, Rama joined with a band of warrior monkeys. They fought the rakshasas for days. Rama finally killed Ravana with a holy arrow. He saved Sita, and they returned to their kingdom.

Vishnu rode an eagle named Garuda.

After the victory, the gods sang Rama's praises from the heavens. Rama ruled over his kingdom. When he died, he was brought to heaven to be with the gods. This myth is still celebrated as Diwali every year.

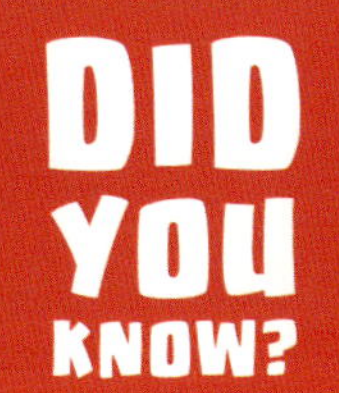

DID YOU KNOW? Vishnu came to earth as Rama to rid the world of rakshasas.

Hinduism is the world's oldest major religion. Its ancient gods, goddesses, and mythologies are still followed today.

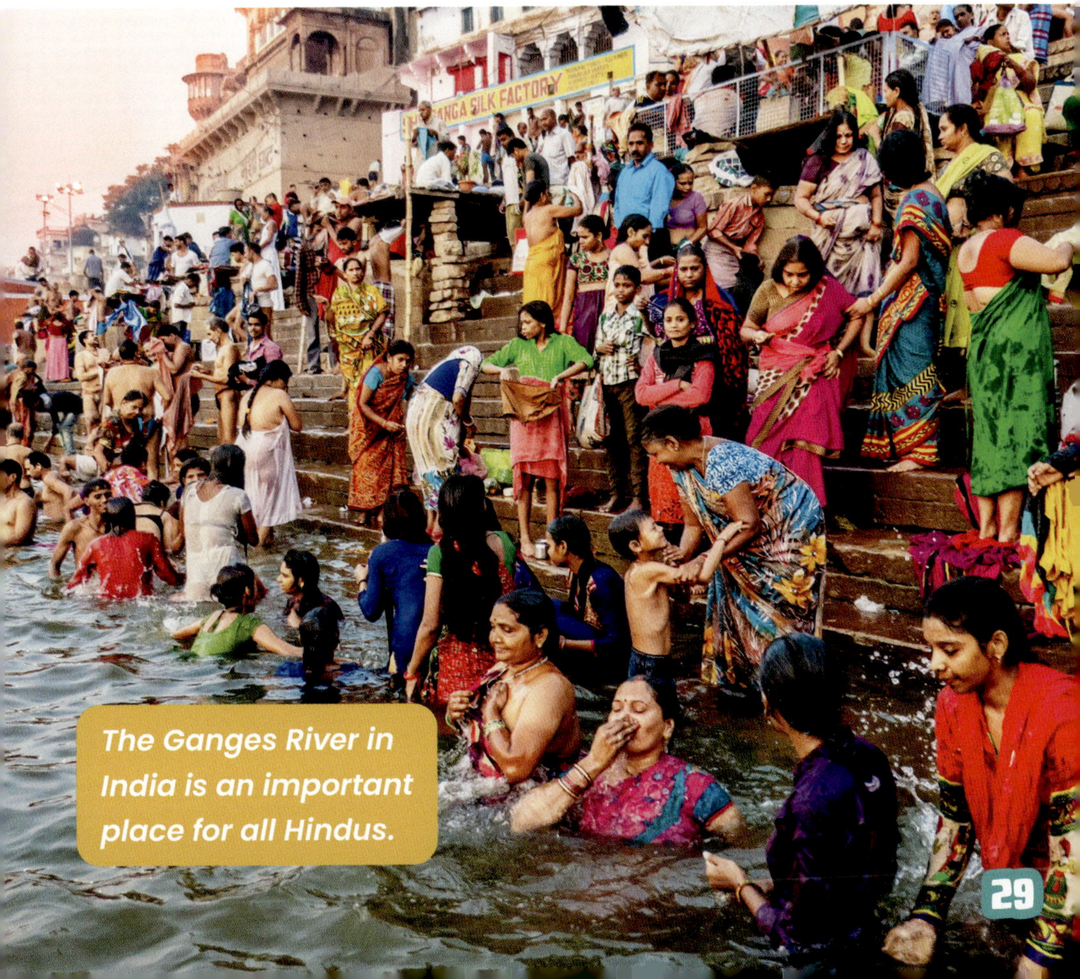

The Ganges River in India is an important place for all Hindus.

MAKING CONNECTIONS

TEXT-TO-SELF

Which form of Brahman do you find most interesting? Please explain your answer.

TEXT-TO-TEXT

Have you read about a different ancient mythology? If so, what did it have in common with Hindu mythology?

TEXT-TO-WORLD

Hinduism and its stories are a part of the oldest religion in the world. Why do you think people have followed the religion for so long?

GLOSSARY

fertility — a woman's ability to have children.

merciful — full of compassion.

pillar — a tall vertical structure.

preserve — to keep safe from harm.

prosperity — success or wealth.

ritual — a religious action performed in a certain way.

supernatural — having to do with forces beyond what is natural.

universe — all existing things, including the Earth and heavens.

worship — to show great honor and respect.

INDEX

This book is filled with videos, puzzles, games, and more! Scan the QR codes* while you read, or visit the website below to make this book pop.

popbooksonline.com/hindu-myth

*Scanning QR codes requires a web-enabled smart device with a QR code reader app and a camera.